MW00473508

Child of The Depression

Growing Up in the 30's & 40's

Sallie Naatz Bailey

Many, many years ago—when I was a little girl—I would travel with my parents to Oswego, NY where my mother grew up and Chittenango, NY —where my father grew up. We would drive through areas where they had lived when they were children and they would point out various houses and recall places and people they had known and things they had done. Most of the time, my reaction ranged from complete disinterest to not even listening. After all, I'd heard it all so many times. I seldom asked questions.

Now they are all gone—everyone of that generation. There's no one to whom I can address my questions. There is so much more I wish I had asked them about the way they lived—the way things were. So that's what I'm doing here. Remembering the fact that my parents' history is—sadly—beyond recall, I will try to tell you the answers before you even ask the questions— about the past that I can recall and what it was like growing up during The Depression and The War Years.

Originally begun as a project for my own family—and posted online as a 'blog' - I found that others—friends and strangers—found it interesting. Those in my age bracket immediately identified with it. What I thought unusual—were the younger people who reacted. All urged me—variously —to have it published (oh right—that's easy) - and to add the other decades that I omitted. One person said it inspired him to write his own 'history' - though he's only in his 40's.

This is not a 'memoir'. It is a history. It's my story and the story of an era, as well. Perhaps, after reading it, you'll feel as though you've visited a different time and place.

For my family
– so they'll know what it was like...

My brother Jack and me - 1932

Child of The Depression
Revised Edition
©2007 Sallie Naatz Bailey

Woodland Studio
sallieb.googlepages.com/

Child of the Depression

GROWING UP IN THE 30'S & 40'S

The Depression. It's always capitalized – and aptly named. The economic misery certainly caused untold mental misery. I won't dwell on that. This is about what it was like growing up in the 30's & 40's.

I was born in 1931 into what many would call fortunate circumstances. My father had a job! He had gone to work for the New York Central Railroad in 1903, (he was 46 when I was born), and had not served in WWI because he was in an essential industry. Thus he had 28 years of seniority by 1931.

We lived in a rented house in Syracuse NY. Many average middle class people rented in those days. Most of the rental houses were owned by the banks, which repossessed them during The Depression when the original owners could no longer make their mortgage payments. Actually we lived in an assortment of rented houses. My mother had a restless soul. She actually *enjoyed* moving—the novelty of a new house—and seemed undaunted by packing and unpacking. With the exception of one house— we always stayed on the North Side so I didn't face the need to change schools.

The first house I remember was what might be called a 'bungalow' - though not in the classic 'arts & crafts' style. A porch spanned the front. Downstairs, there was a living room (no fireplace), dining room and a kitchen that could contain a small table at its center. A utility room off the kitchen was where the refrigerator lived. Many people still had ice boxes so this was quite a luxury. Ours was a General Electric model with a cylindrical coil on top.

A back door off this area led to a small back porch. There was a hall with stairs leading from the kitchen to the side door and cellar. A 'milk box' with access from inside and outside occupied a place in the wall beside the door. It was here that the milkman made his delivery.

The milk came in glass bottles. It was pasteurized but not homogenized so the cream rose to the top. The bottle was shaped like a modified 'hourglass', with the cream settling in the top where it could be easily poured off to use in coffee.

The cellar itself was not 'finished' - not a 'game room'. It was just a cellar - with a furnace squatting in the middle - its ductwork spreading across the ceiling like the arms of a giant octopus. This creature was fed by the coal dumped down a chute into a coal bin - a room-like area built with rough, unfinished wood. The coal truck drove in the driveway, put the chute through the window in the coal bin and made its delivery with a house shaking roar! There were no thermostats or automatic anything. At night in cold weather, the coal furnaces were 'banked' and on winter mornings, we would be awakened by the reverberating sound of the ashes being 'shook down'. We would hustle to get dressed in the only warm room in the whole house – the bathroom! When the door was shut it heated rapidly because it was small.

The hot water tank had a pilot light that had to be lit when you wanted hot water. It was not automatic. It was lighted to do laundry, dishes & for baths. Woe betide the family who left the house without making certain the hot water tank was turned off. One time we did forget and I will never forget what ensued. Upon returning someone went to use the bathroom, flushed the toilet – and the water was boiling hot and steaming! We turned off the heater and opened all the faucets to let the hissing steam and hot water run off. A bit longer and the hot water tank might have exploded, taking off like a missile!

Next to the coal bin, there was usually another such 'room' with wooden shelves and it was here that the home canned fruits and vegetables were stored. My mother's specialties were stewed tomatoes, chili sauce and strawberry jam. She called it 'putting up' - vegetables, jams, whatever. Sometimes she did peaches—both canned and in the form of jam. I never did like chili sauce but—oh—the fragrance. It was wonderful to come

5

home from school and smell that wonderful spicy smell.

The washing machine stood by the set tubs with its wringing mechanism attached to the top. There were no timers - the clothes would agitate till someone came to stop the machine and drain the water into the set tub. They were then fed into the wringer by hand. We kids were warned off with lurid stories about what happened to children foolish enough to get their fingers too close to the wringer!

Upstairs there were three bedrooms and one bath - the *only* bathroom. As well as other essential plumbing, it contained a tub with four claw shaped feet - no shower. The bathrooms were almost always black & white (just as kitchens were almost always cream colored). Four bedrooms weren't common. During those Depression days most people had no more than two children - and there were many one child and even no-children marriages. Except for devout Catholics, that is - and even they were sometimes suspiciously infertile...

There was always an attic - inhabited by boxes, dust, wasps and assorted ghosties & ghoulies in a child's imagination. Definitely a place to be avoided - so it was where the Christmas presents were always stashed. The attic space also served as wonderful insulation - keeping the small houses warmer in winter & cooler in summer.

Unlike today's suburbs, every neighborhood had sidewalks. It was where we rode our tricycles - and later - our two wheelers. Not in the road. Never. Even though those quiet streets saw very little traffic.

The Drama

Every good story should have some drama—and so it is with this 'story'. I'm not sure how much is actual memory and how much is the result of frequent re-telling by my parents. My memory of the events following the incident are vague. What I do remember clearly is that my mother was in the upstairs front bedroom. I was told that she was changing to go somewhere and was keeping an eye on me from that vantage point. What follows, I can see vividly in my mind—I was in my little red wagon on the sidewalk in front of the house, one knee in the wagon and the other leg poised to push—when I saw my mother in the upstairs window. I remember thinking that it was remarkable that she was in full view, wearing only her slip. She was screaming in a tone of voice I had never heard— *"Sallie—get out of the cart*—**NOW**—run– come here– **NOW**—run!"* The words were a jumbled sequence.

Luckily for me, I had two factors working to my advantage— the panic in her voice - and the fact that children of that era were taught to 'mind' without argument. *I jumped and ran.*

I have no recollection of the immediate events that followed. I do know that—by all accounts—my mother had happened to look out the window, checking on me—and saw a car that had been parked about four houses up the hill—diagonally across the street—starting to roll. The wheels were turned outward— toward me. A few seconds after I jumped and ran, my little red wagon was crushed under its wheels and it came to rest against a tree just beyond. For many years, the trunk of that tree bore the scars on its bark.

The couple who lived in the house were, of course, appalled by what might have happened (the car belonged to a visitor). They came to our house one day soon after, bearing a gift—a new wagon to replace my old one. I remember that it was blue and cream colored (not red) and bigger —with a 'streamlined' design—and when I 'pushed' it with one foot, the wheels didn't move as easily as those on my little red wagon. I never liked it as well.

Playtime

Every child—boy or girl—had such a wagon (we called them 'carts'), but—curiously—it was mostly boys who had scooters. A scooter looked like today's skateboards—but with a vertical rod and a wooden or metal

handlebar across the top. Those things could go! Our roller skates were downright primitive, compared to today's 'in-line' skates. They consisted of a metal 'platform' with clamps, front and back. These would clamp onto the soles of our shoes and then be tightened with a 'key'. Leather straps across the foot secured them. As I recall, they had to be oiled occasionally, too - to keep them running smoothly.

We all had Kiddy Kars, graduated to tricycles and

from there—to full size two wheel bikes. I don't recall training wheels at all—at least I never had them. My father taught me to ride on the sidewalk in front of our house. He would run along beside the rear wheel, steadying the bike till I stopped. One day, I stopped, dismounted and looked around for my Dad. He was standing in front of our house! I was both appalled and excited! I had done it! I had ridden alone—without help!

My mother never had dolls when she was a child. She and her siblings considered themselves quite lucky to have food on the table. So she had her dolls vicariously—through me. I had beautiful dolls—the kind that today are hunted so avidly by collectors. Those dolls are especially prized today if they've never been removed from their boxes! Pity the poor child who receives such a doll.

Mine were well played with—but I was reasonably careful. I think the joy my mother took in them made me more respectful of them. Nonetheless—they were dressed, undressed and their hair was mussed in the process.

There was Dy-dee—the baby doll that took water through the mouth and then 'peed' in the tiny diaper. Betsy-Wetsy was another name for that type of doll. I had By-Lo Baby—with its face resembling that of a newborn, a Charlie McCarthy doll with a mouth that moved - just like the original - a beautiful baby doll that wore an exquisite lace dress over a pink satin under-dress, a Princess Elizabeth doll with a little tiara, a Deanna Durbin (a singing star of the era) doll with dark hair and yellow organdy dress trimmed with black velvet ribbon. All of them were acquired over a period of years.

The prize—the one I loved best—was my *Wendy Ann*. There was a well known toy store in Syracuse at the time—known as The Condé Toy Shop. Every time we were downtown, we would walk by and look in the windows—a favorite treat. One day—I saw the unimaginable—the doll I knew would never be mine—Wendy Anne. She came in a *suitcase* with many changes of clothes—sort of a pre-cursor to today's Barbie— but she was a *little girl*. Her clothing was fabulous—a pink organdy dance dress, a white pique 'golfing' dress trimmed with red and accompanied by a little golf stick, a 'party' dress of aqua organdy trimmed with lace, a pair of jodhpurs with little riding boots, a navy blue 'sailor' coat and a red sailor jacket. There was much more—changes of underwear, nightclothes, shoes, hats…. She was beautiful—my dream. I knew I would never possess her—she was a Madame Alexander doll and my mother had said she was too expensive—but just 'visiting' her in the shop window was enough.

That Christmas—Wendy Ann was under the tree. I have never forgotten her - or the pure magic of that moment. Many, many years later—my husband gave me an incredibly sweet birthday gift. He had seen a contemporary Madame Alexander doll in a shop—labeled "Wendy". It was a 'collectible' doll. I'm not a doll collector but he bought it and gave it to me—because of the name. She lives under a glass dome in the bedroom—a reminder of my much loved Wendy Ann.

However many toys we had—and we didn't have that many— we were like children today. That is—if we were left to our own devices—we created the most wonderful playthings from empty boxes, cast off clothes and our imaginations.

In the 30's and 40's, there were vacant lots in every neighborhood – lots on which nothing had been built and which were overgrown with weeds. There was one across the street from our house. In those days, it was perfectly safe for little girls to play in those empty lots – with weeds that grew higher than our heads. My friend, Nancy - who lived a block away - and I played there endlessly, tromping down the tall weeds to make "rooms" and "hallways" in make-believe houses. We punched holes in the metal lids of jars and fearlessly captured bumble bees, grasshoppers, crickets and butterflies.

The weeds were pretty much leveled on the empty lots used by groups of little boys playing softball. There were no 'Little Leagues' for baseball - or 'Pop Warner' leagues for football. The rules were established by fiat —'this is 1st base and that's outside', etc. If "Skinny" wasn't a good player, he'd get five strikes instead of three. It was the best of times for little boys.

Summer evenings, we'd stay out late—often under the street lights—playing Hide 'n' Seek, Tag, King of the Hill, Kick the Can, Blind Man's Buff....

The Neighborhood

In every neighborhood, there was a 'corner store' (they were always on a corner) – in our neighborhood, it was a tiny place called Dan's. It was owned by Dan Delargy, whose son was named after him and called "Junior" – a very common nickname in those years. Junior was older and didn't hang around with us "little kids".

Periodically, I would be given a penny – or even two – and it was off to Dan's to squander the windfall. A penny in the '30's bought a lot of candy – and oh that wonderful array of penny candy behind the slanting glass that shielded the wooden display case. There were little tins that contained pastel colored creamy candy that you would eat with a tiny metal spoon that accompanied it. There were wax bottles filled with sweet syrup and strips with colorful candy 'buttons' on them – and Dubble Bubble Gum, each one wrapped in a little comic strip inside the outer wrapping. A nickel was a bonanza –kid heaven – and Dan never seemed to lose patience with us. He was a benign presence behind the counter. In summer, we bought popsicles and fudgesicles. Rarely, one would have the word "free" inscribed on the wooden stick. That meant that a free fudgesicle was yours. Bliss!

In winter we wore woolen coats and snow pants with 'overshoes' that pulled on over our shoes and buckled. They were waterproof but not lined and when our feet would get so cold they'd start to itch —it was time to come in! Great clots of snow would cling like pom-poms to the woolen pants. I would remove my boots and my mother would stand me on the register to warm up—with the snow pants still on. The smell of wet wool would permeate the house.

10

There were still horse drawn wagons traveling the paved streets, leaving the mark of their passing in the form of a ribbon of horse manure down the center of the street. One such cart belonged to the 'rag man'. He bought and sold rags and about once a week, his wagon would come clanking and clopping down the street, as he called "Raa-a-aags... raa-a-aags..." in a monotonous sing-song. I remember that I always thought he was calling "Eggs...". If I was in the small front yard when he came by, I ran like mad for the back yard because he scared me. Another such 'entrepreneur' was the man who shuffled through the neighborhood with a large wheel-like apparatus strapped on his back. He was the man who sharpened scissors. These were often men who had lost their relatively well paying jobs as a result of The Depression.

Out of work men took any job they could get. The cliché is selling apples on the street—but in fact—more men went door to door selling shoelaces and such services as that mentioned above. One such occupation was taking photographs of people on city streets and then approaching the subject and handing them a card telling them how to order the prints.

This photo of Jack, me & Dad, taken on Salina St. in downtown Syracuse— 1938 or '39—was just such a photo. Jack is carrying a Wells & Coverly box containing his new suit. I'm the only one who has spotted the street photographer and—if you look closely at the hands— mine is slightly blurred. It appears that—in my interest—I had just dropped my Dad's hand. Note the lollipop! My father ordered a print of the picture— much to my mother's disgust. Today—I treasure it.

Since there have been suburbs, people have made sport of the fact that the houses are so close together. What?! We have such short memories? The houses in city neighborhoods were separated by no more than the width of a driveway - and where there was no driveway, they were often separated by no more than six feet. This was often referred at as an 'alley' and was usually lined with pebbles. The garage was in the farthest corner of the back yard. It was one car with a door that swung open. After the war, when bigger cars started coming out, people often had to 'bump out' the back of the garage to accommodate their greater length. Most just added a bump-out big enough to accept the snout of the car. After all, why waste money? Nobody wasted money during The Depression.

The way we were...

As a little girl in the '30's, I did not wear slacks or overalls. I wore dresses - frumpy little numbers that looked like miniatures of the house-dresses that our mothers wore. They were flowered cotton with Peter Pan collars and short, puffed sleeves. Since little girls then were like little girls now - i.e. they ran, jumped and played just as vigorously and fell often on gravel driveways and rough sidewalks - I went through my early years with scraped, scabby knees. Sometimes my mother couldn't pick all the embedded gravel out so there were always a few bluish shadows under the skin. The only consolation was that boys suffered the same fate. They had to wear short pants till they were about ten or twelve! The only time I wore long pants was when we went to the Adirondack Mountains where the weather was cool and bugs were plentiful.

But -ah - the party dresses. They were organdy or some similar diaphanous material - pastel and/or flowered and accessorized with shining Mary Jane patent leather shoes. I was very fortunate - my mother never made me wear the ugly oxford tie shoes so many little girls wore - I had 'everyday' Mary Janes. The difference was that they were not patent leather, often had a T-strap and were usually scuffed.

Grammar School...

...as it was called – not "Elementary" – was an adventure. We walked to school of course – though I doubt that I did during Kindergarten. I don't really recall that part of it but the school was about a mile from my home. My memory of kindergarten itself is vivid. The teacher was a little, sweet faced, soft spoken woman with gray hair. She wore pinafores and a ribbon in her hair every day. Often the ribbon was red. Her name was Miss Driscoll. Her assistant was Miss Davis, a tall, reserved woman with dark hair.

The school was Salem Hyde and it was 'new' - only ten years old. Most of the teachers had arrived at the school right out of college – or 'Normal School' as teachers' colleges were called then – and were therefore relatively young, though we all thought they were old. Most were unmarried – not uncommon for schoolteachers in those days. We were not, after all, so far from the era when all female teachers were required to be unmarried! There were no male teachers in our school. Incidentally —there were separate entrances for the boys and girls—at opposite ends of the school!

Kindergarten is a montage of memories – there were the mats that were unrolled from the low cupboards for rest time. Many of the children actually slept but I never did – I never went to sleep easily and don't to this day. There are memories of gathering around the piano while Miss Davis played and Miss Driscoll led us in such songs as "Home on the Range" (at the word 'range' I pictured a kitchen stove – or 'range' as stoves were then often called) –"where the deer and the antelope play." Confusion reigned again in my mind as I tried to picture 'cantaloupe" frolicking.

The best memory of all was the paints – large jars of poster paints. I can still remember the smell when they were opened – and kneeling on the floor painting pictures on large sheets of newsprint spread out before us. Wonderful! I think that my eventual career as an artist was presaged in the enthusiasm with which I painted then. I do know that all through grammar school, I was always assigned to work on backdrops for the various plays and pageants – and was excused from class to do so. I recall one project that involved painting huge covered wagons – though I'll be darned if I can remember the play itself.

One that I *do* remember was *The Wedding of the Flowers*. The shortest girl and boy in the class were selected to be the bride and groom. The rest of us were attendants. Since I was – always and forever – one of the taller or tallest girls in the class, I was a sunflower and stood in the last row. How I longed to be a rose – but alas – *I was never a rose...*

13

The principal was Miss Mary Lawlor. I remember her as very tall. She may not have been tall, but she was a commanding, gaunt figure with her gray hair pulled back in a bun and always clad in a sweeping, floor length black cape— lined with purple—that swirled about her as she walked – stalked? – through the halls.

Every day at mid- morning, we were served Ritz crackers and milk. A half pint of white milk was five cents – chocolate milk was seven cents. In those Depression years, a snack was not looked upon lightly. There was no cafeteria. We either brought a brown bag lunch or – if we lived close enough – went home for lunch. At various times, I did both.

Much later – when I went to Lincoln Junior High School – not "Middle School" in those days – I remember going back to Salem Hyde for Girl Scout meetings. What I most remember was the smell. The halls of Lincoln School smelled like dirty gym shoes and those of Salem Hyde were suffused with the fragrance of the young teachers' perfume!

My Aunt's Camp in the Adirondacks

The camp—called *Camp Forestview*—near Limekiln Lake, in the Adirondacks, had only a wood stove for heat - no electricity, no running water - and no indoor plumbing— only an 'outhouse' that was the perfect inducement for constipation. The camp had been built as a hunter's cabin in 1914 and was little changed from that era by the time my family started going there. The bedroom partitions went part way up to the ceiling so when someone had to get up in the night and use the big white chamber pots under the beds – the whole world knew. The roof was tin & if it rained in the night, it "would wake the dead", as my mother often said. We were never quite sure if what we were hearing was rain on the roof or someone using the chamber pot! If it didn't stop—it was rain.

To get water, we had to carry buckets across the dirt road and take a path down to the spring. I remember my father coming back, carrying those

14

 sloshing buckets. The spring water was ice cold and pure. My father and uncle had made a dam of stones with a pipe—probably lead —running through it, so the water came gushing out as though from a spigot that was never turned off. Two of the stones, arranged in an unintentional 'seat' configuration at one side, became my 'throne'. The spring was a favorite playground. I and a little friend spent endless hours there, creating castles, mansions and cabins in our minds. Sometimes we would imagine creatures in the dark woods that stretched off behind the spring, the forbidden area where we had been instructed never to venture. Ultimately, this self-created terror would send us running pell-mell up the curving path that led to the road and safety.

My aunt was a teetotaler and so my Dad, who was not much of a drinker himself, would buy a six pack of beer and leave it in the icy pool beneath the pipe. My uncle seemed to spend an inordinate amount of time fetching water when we were there. He was a slight, gentle man with snowy white hair and an ever present pipe, his soft-spoken words weighted with a heavy German accent. I'm told that he spoke several languages, but English was obviously not his best. As a small child, I was fascinated by him and followed him around, talking constantly. Periodically he would murmur "Ja... ja..." his soft, contemplative voice drawing out the words. My mother was sure he didn't understand a word of what I was saying. Next to the camp was a 'yard' full of ferns where the chipmunks lived. Telling me to be very still – a challenge for a young child - he could coax them out with peanuts and they would eat out of his hand, climbing into his palm in their eagerness.

My mother never liked it very much up there. She disliked the very things I loved — the smell of wood smoke from the stove and kerosene from the lamps, the fact that the only evening entertainment was a card

15

game in the dim light of those lamps, with cards sliding across the slippery surface of the oil cloth that covered the big kitchen table.

She disliked going to bed early because the lack of light made it difficult to do almost anything else. She disliked sharing the same bed with me while my father shared the other room with my brother, complaining that my squirming disturbed her sleep. Most of all, she disliked the rainy days when all of us were penned up inside the two small, dark rooms that comprised the first floor and we children would crank up the ancient Victrola. Old, scratchy records by Enrico Caruso and other opera luminaries would speed through the introductory notes and then grind down to a gradually slowing moan, until we cranked it up again.

 It never seemed odd to me that my mother was willing to make the trek to The Woods year after year despite such 'grinding down' of her nerves and my bouts with car sickness. The first car I remember was our 1932 Buick Coupe - with room for 2 passengers in the front and two in the 'rumble seat'. The rumble seat was where the trunk of contemporary cars is located - and it opened, swinging down to reveal the seat. This was where my brother rode - with our English setter, Eugene. My mother drove - my father never learned how and never wanted to learn! I rode on his lap. Remember - no seat belts - no *anything* of a safety nature. Actually - the winding roads and slower speeds of the era created their own safety! Because of my carsickness, we had to make so many stops along the way —my father and I walking along the road while Mother crept the car forward—that my brother said that Dad wound up walking half way to the Adirondacks!

We continued to go to the camp through the war years. Gas was rationed and we had to come by train because there wasn't enough fuel to allow us to drive almost one hundred miles from home. My uncle would meet us in his ancient Hudson motor car. It was in pristine condition. He probably didn't add much more mileage each year than what it took to drive to the camp in July and back to their home again in September.

One summer, when we arrived, we discovered that, in our winter absence, power lines had been strung down the road and the camp had been wired for electricity! I think I was the only member of the family who was saddened by this 'progress'. It would never be the same again without those flickering, smelly kerosene lamps with the mantels that had to be replaced if they were scorched; the lamps that created a flickering parade of shadows on the wall as we carefully carried them up the stairs, lighting our way to bed.

We continued our treks to my aunt's camp throughout my teen years – even a couple of times after I was married. Now there are only a few black and white photographs of those happy years left and they carry certain poignancy. Many of the people in the pictures are dead—my aunt and uncle, father and mother… my brother. The album still contains them, laughing, wearing the now strange clothing of the time, my brother in knickers and argyle socks. They posed with friends by the Buick coupe - my father standing on the left - my mother poising me on the edge of the open rumble seat—the others positioned in, on and around the car - all smiling.

In the camp's later incarnations, after my cousin inherited the place, it acquired running water and indoor plumbing and, furnished with pleasant comfortable furniture, it assumed a gentility quite removed from the rustic, shabby air of the early years. The smoke stained open board walls on which successive visitors and family members had scrawled their names, the date and remarks—a sort of structural guest book and diary — were covered over with pine paneling. The evidence of their stay - their existence—was buried…

Girl Scouts & Summer Camp

It must have been around 1940 when our Salem Hyde School Girl Scout troop was asked to serve as 'hostesses' at a reception for a noted Chinese woman aviator at the old Syracuse Museum of Fine Arts. I remember being so fascinated with the beautiful silk coats we wore that I hated to take mine off. It was emerald green with lovely embroidery! (I am second from the right in the photograph).

Woman Flier Greets Ushers at Chinese Art Exhibition

Shown with Miss Lee ya-Ching, China's "first woman of the air," are Miss Pauline Eallonardo, left, and Miss Ellen Virdin, right, standing with Miss Lee in front row. In the second row are Misses Charlene Lammers, Ann Mawhinney, Katherine Kellogg, Sallie Naatz and Marilsa Frey, all ushers at the Chinese display in the Museum of Fine Arts.

One summer, I spent *two weeks* at the Girl Scout camp - ironically named Camp Hoover—located on Song Lake in Tully, NY just south of Syracuse. It was quite an event. We were given a list of things to bring with us. My mother and I worked together on the storage unit to go at the head of the cot. They were all the same - we picked up a wooden orange crate at the local market, put it on end and fashioned a fabric skirt secured around the top by elastic. The crates had a partition that formed a 'shelf' within.

I loved Girl Scout Camp and was never homesick - I was with my grammar school friends. I'm not clear on this but I may have gone for two summers. At any rate, it was wonderful. Our 'troop' was housed four girls to a tent, and the tents were arranged in a circle. One tent was occupied by the counselors - who were teens at the time. To us, they were practically 'grown-ups'.

We had swimming lessons by the waterfront docks - which had various roped off areas for different levels of prowess. Our levels were designated by the color of our swim caps. Red caps were for rank beginners. I started at that level and never moved beyond the second level (green cap) - but it was there that I learned to float, do the doggy paddle and a 'sort of' passable sidestroke.

Meals were served in the dining hall - a wooden structure. The food was nothing like that served to my husband at the pricey private boys' camp *he* attended as a child - but we were not overly concerned - as long as we could buy candy bars and assorted treats at the commissary. One thing I *do* remember is being introduced to 'powdered eggs' for breakfast. *Yuck.* Even the biscuits made with powdered eggs tasted terrible!

We loved receiving letters from home and on Sunday - the parents came to visit. One night we did what I believe all campers tried sooner or later. Word was passed from tent to tent. After dark and 'lights out' - the plan was to sneak out, crawl past the councilors' tent to the access road and from there head to the main road. Where *exactly* we thought we would go from there I don't know.

That night - with much rustling, whispering and muffled giggles - we slipped out of our tents and *crawled,* hitching along on our bellies. We made it to the access road - I *think* we were *allowed* to reach it - and there - dead ahead were our councilors' legs, blocking our path as they stood, hands on hips. Bummer! *How did they ever guess??* I don't know about the others but I was relieved to see them!!

Staying Healthy

My generation, and those that preceded it, lived in fear - not of nuclear bombs or terrorist attacks - but fear of sickness. Even such 'minor' ailments as strep throat could lead to death. Sulpha had been developed in the thirties, (and was widely used on the wounds of soldiers during World War II), but we had no penicillin or other antibiotics of its class. Scarlet fever would sometimes develop from untreated strep infections and, for the most unfortunate - progress into rheumatic fever which could damage heart valves or kill. Survivors often lived out lives limited by damaged heart valves and there was no such thing as open heart surgery or valve replacement. Most people of my generation vividly remember overly cautious mothers hovering over us when we were sick.

We had a vaccine for small pox - but none for DPT - diphtheria, pertussis (whooping cough) and Typhoid or for measles or chicken pox. None for flu. There was none for polio - called infantile paralysis because it afflicted mostly children. That disease usually occurred in the summer - and every few years there would be an epidemic which would cause cancellations - as mentioned above - and a state of panic in parents. It was a crippling, killing disease and few knew that our president -

19

Franklin Roosevelt - could not walk without assistance because of his bout with the disease. It was known that he had had it as a young man, and in fact, he was nominal head of the March of Dimes - a fundraising effort to find a 'cure'. Each year there would be a drive and even the theaters would turn on the lights between the double features in order to pass the collection box to the audience.

A year or two after my adventure at Girl Scout camp, I attended a local Catholic camp called Lourdes - I may have been the only person there who was not Catholic. I went with two neighborhood friends who attended the Parochial School. There we had the magnificent luxury of *wood cabins* and *bunk beds!* There was a Catholic service every evening in the chapel. Each evening when the bells would sound to summon us - the Catholic girls would remove the screen and pile out the back window of the cabin - apparently their version of the 'sneaking out' at Girl Scout camp. I thought that was *terrible* - and dutifully trotted off with those who were attending!

Our good time was cut short by a ***polio epidemic***. The much dreaded, crippling disease - which primarily afflicted children - was raging in the Syracuse area. At that time, no one had any idea what caused it - only that there was no way to prevent it and no effective treatment. Theories abounded - but avoidance of crowds and beaches was the prescribed course of action. Much to our disappointment, we were all sent home from Lourdes a week early. It would be many years later - in the 1950's - that the church bells and fire sirens were sounded at noon throughout the city of Syracuse - announcing that Jonas Salk's serum had been found effective. As a young parent at that time, I remember that tears welled in my eyes when I heard that sound.

Tuberculosis was unchecked and unpreventable. Treatment consisted of diet, rest & fresh air - preferably in a sanitarium in the mountains. Removal of part of the lung was often the only recourse. My brother contracted it when he was four years old from a relative who later died from the disease. He was treated successfully at home. (My father's sister suffered from it in the second decade of the twentieth century and spent a couple of years at Dr. Trudeau's sanitarium in Saranac Lake. In the 1890's my father's *sister, brother and mother* - all - had died of tuberculosis. In school - every year - we had a "TB" needle test - pinpricks that would turn red and swell if the germ was in our body. A 'positive' didn't necessarily mean that the disease was present - only that the person had been exposed to it. A positive result meant an anguished period of waiting for testing and results.

The New York Central Railroad – and Its Role in Our Life

My father's father emigrated from Prussia in about 1870. Like many German immigrants of the time, his goal was to work on the railroad. He settled - and raised his family in Chittenango Station, New York. It was there that he built his own home and farmed while working on the railroad. His four sons, including my father, all went to work for the New York Central Railroad as soon as they were old enough to do so.

My father was devoted to the railroad. His attitude toward 'his train' was much like that of a sea captain toward his ship. Indeed, some of the men - whom he supervised as a conductor and who liked and respected him - called him "Captain". He retired only when he was forced to by law after more than fifty years of service.

Syracuse, New York was known as the city where the railroad ran through the streets. The new art deco station with elevated tracks replaced the old downtown station in 1936 – when I was five years old. It was - and is - a marvel of Art Deco architecture. The photo of me shown here was taken in a *Fotomat* booth in the new station.

That 1936 station was later replaced by a new facility in an outlying area. The Art Deco station was then desecrated by a faux modern front extension and was used as a Greyhound Bus station for several decades during which it endured much deterioration. It was completely restored in 2003 for use as a television news studio by Time Warner. A local artist painted a mural depicting those past times on what was the platform wall. It now faces the four lane commuter highway that replaced the elevated tracks. A call went out for photos. I sent a picture of my father, who is now part of that mural.

My father's 'route' started in Buffalo, ran to New York and back to Buffalo. Technically, we should have lived in Buffalo because my father rode as a passenger (they called it 'dead-heading) to Buffalo to start his run and at its conclusion, he reversed the procedure back to Syracuse. People did not pull up roots casually in those days, so we remained in Syracuse.

This procedure had one advantage for me. Several times, when my Dad's train came into the station en route from New York City to Buffalo, my mother and I would meet it. I would board, to be met by my Dad. He seated me and then proceeded to attend to his duties, checking on me occasionally. Upon reaching Buffalo, he and I would disembark into the station, where he would go to his locker and do whatever mysterious rites he had to perform - putting some things in and taking others out. Then we would re-board the train for the return to Syracuse. In later years I would say that I was - perhaps - the only person who made many trips to Buffalo and never set foot outside the station!

Dad would sit with me on the return trip and do paperwork while I would usually read. We'd arrive at the station late at night to be met by my mother. I loved those trips, I loved the trains - the smell and sound of them - the frightening moment when the huge steam engine would huff into view and we would step back from the edge of the platform with a mixture of awe and fear. I will always be a *railroad brat.*

Our Extended Family

My mother, Aunt Ethel, Momma & Uncle Ed with son, Edward

The two most important figures, outside my immediate family, were my mother's sister, Aunt Ethel - and my mother's mother, my grandmother. We all called her Momma— including my father. Momma was my only living grandparent; the others had died before I was born. Momma lived with us intermittently but most of the time she preferred to have her own

22

Barbara Weiss
Susan Weiss
Sallie
Gene

Gene adored being pushed around the block in my doll carriage. Here we are with two little neighbor girls. At right – our cat, Butch, 'watches' our 10" Philco TV (with record player built in)!

small apartment. She came for dinner almost every Sunday and—of course—was present for all holidays. She was a small woman with a slight build and a very quiet, lady-like demeanor. I never heard her speak in a loud voice or in an angry manner. We spent every Christmas Eve with my mother's sister, Aunt Ethel—and her husband, my Uncle Clinton. On Christmas Day they came to our house.

My mother had three brothers whom we saw occasionally but she was not as close to them. My father had three surviving siblings - two sisters and a brother—all of whom lived in Chittenango—a town about fifteen miles away. We visited them with somewhat more frequency—though we never joined them for holidays. It was one of the sisters - and her husband - who owned the camp in the Adirondacks.

Our Pets

We always had pets—always a dog and cat. The English setter, Gene, was the first

dog I remember. We often called him 'Goofy' - because he *was* - *h*e was a clown who adored attention and loved riding in the rumble seat of our Buick coupe. He'd sit next to my brother with his ears flying in the wind and his tongue hanging out— my brother wasn't happy when I said it was hard to tell them apart...

He was followed by a collie I named Lad, a result of my 'tween' devotion to the author, Albert Payson Terhune and his books about his

23

beloved collies. After Lad came Sandy—a rust-colored Cocker Spaniel.

We had two cats as I was growing up. The first was a gray and white cat that was killed by a car in front of our house. We got the second around 1942. He came from the SPCA and turned out to be half Persian. He had rickets because he was separated from the mother cat too soon—so his front legs were bowed and he appeared to always be walking downhill! We named him "Butch" - a misnomer if ever there was one! He was never allowed outside and lived a long, pampered life till well after I was married in 1954. The pets provided comfort and companionship through all the rigors of The Depression and The War Years.

The Holidays

The holiday traditions are part of every generation's memories. We entertained family for dinner on Easter, Thanksgiving and Christmas. My mother preferred to entertain on those days, rather than *be* entertained - which suited me just fine. Especially on Christmas.

The holiday started officially, then as now, after Thanksgiving - except that decorations didn't go up *anywhere* till then. My mother always made fruitcake. It had the reputation of being excellent (she was a fine cook) but I never liked it. I did love the fragrance that accompanied it, however - all the wonderful spices. After the ritual of making it was done, my mother would soak the loaves of fruitcake in brandy, wrap them in dish towels and let them 'age' for a month in the dining room buffet. Sometimes she would 'hide' small boxed Christmas presents in the buffet - usually those from the Addis Company that came already secured with ribbon. For many years, I thought that those boxes were actually scented with that heady, holiday fragrance!

This is one of those magical silver Addis Company boxes that – for some reason – survived and which I still have.

E. W. Edwards department store had a fabulous toy department across the street from the main store. In addition to the street access, the 'annex' could be reached via a

24

tunnel from the basement floor of the store. It ran under the street and was a boon in our snowy Central New York winters. As a child, I was fascinated by *the tunnel!* I remember the toy annex as two large rooms. During the Christmas season, a train ran around the perimeter of the ceiling on something like a monorail. Children could ride in it - and you could see their happy faces as they waved down at the people below. Unfortunately, by the time it was installed, I was too big to be able to ride in it.

At home, the live tree was purchased and put up one week before Christmas. It was *always* a Balsam with that wonderful fragrance that has meant Christmas to me ever since. My father centered the tree in a bucket called a coal scuttle and proceeded to fill the bucket with coal. It was then placed in a corner and the top of the tree was secured to the molding with heavy string, tacked into place. We seldom placed the tree in front of a window because - in those days - trees were not pruned into beautiful, thick 'triangles' There was always a 'bald' spot (only one if we were lucky and very selective) which was turned toward the wall.

The tree remained, unadorned, in its bare scuttle full of coal - till Christmas Eve. My parents trimmed it *after* I went to bed. When I came downstairs on Christmas morning - there was this magical vision - splendid with its lights, ornaments and tinsel. *Santa had decorated the tree!!* That's one tradition that my husband and I would *not* carry on when we had our own family. Our tree was decorated after we put it up. I believe it had something to do with the fact that "some assembly required" was a virtually unknown phrase in those days.

I don't remember when I stopped believing in Santa - it was just an evolution. My brother - who was ten years older - certainly deserved credit for not spoiling the fantasy for me. I think - perhaps - that my first intimation occurred when I lay awake at night and heard the mysterious sound of feet making trip after trip to the attic and back down the stairs!

The Christmas stocking was always secured to my bedpost - even long after I stopped 'believing'. My mother still managed to fill it while I was asleep. For many years, it was an old nylon stocking of hers. The trinkets within were wrapped in plain white tissue paper - as were the presents under the tree - but those were secured with plain red ribbon. I had strict orders that I could open my stocking but must not get out of bed till I heard my parents moving about. The stocking was always topped with a comic book and - since I was an avid reader - that kept me occupied despite my excitement.

Later in the day, Aunt Ethel, Uncle Clinton and Momma would arrive for the traditional Christmas dinner. In addition to the turkey, one item that was *never omitted* from the table was:

My Mother's Cranberry Relish
1 bag of raw cranberries
2 oranges cut up - skin and all
about 1 cup sugar
Grind (process today) all together and refrigerate!

Today - the 1 lb. bag of cranberries has been *downsized* - like almost everything else - to 12 ounces- so I use one *large* orange.

Entertainment

There were many neighborhood theaters. The one within walking distance of our house was The Palace Theater in Eastwood. Every Saturday afternoon, my friends and I walked to ***The Palace*** with our ten cent admission clutched in our hands. (During the war years—a tax was levied—admission went to eleven cents and later—to twelve).

Each matinee had a feature film, a second feature (called a 'B' movie), a newsreel, short subject, coming attractions and—if we were lucky—more than one cartoon! The main drawing card though—was the Saturday matinee serial—featuring such well known characters as space traveler, Buck Rogers, and other super heroes. These were an ongoing 'continued' feature.

The theaters in downtown Syracuse included the rococo Loews State Theater—a veritable palace of Moorish elegance and the rather more modest RKO Keiths. There was the Eckel, the Paramount, the Strand (where a period of briefly resurgent vaudeville acts played) - and many lesser theaters such as the Riviera and Empire.

Loews and Keiths always had first run pictures. During the '30s and '40s, they charged thirty five cents admission during the day and sixty five cents at night. When I was in High School and also when we all worked summers during school vacation, we would meet friends downtown on a Friday night and go to the movies, taking the bus both ways. There was no risk for young women alone at eleven PM or later on the downtown streets.

Entertainment at home consisted of the radio, the record player that played the old '78's and reading. There was no television until 1945. Because my brother was a teen-ager when I was a kindergartener, the music I heard most often was that of the Big Bands: Glenn Miller, Tommy Dorsey, Benny Goodman, Artie Shaw - all the 'greats' of that era. Radio was Bob Hope, Jack Benny, Fred Allen, Fibber McGee and Molly - too many to list.

My parents were not 'readers' so my taste in books and magazines was also formed by my brother. As a result, I went straight from comic books to Time and Life magazines. Colliers, Saturday Evening Post - even Esquire - were the magazines with which I was familiar. I never went through a movie magazine/women's magazine stage.

Before I learned to read, my father would sit by my bed each night and read to me. The books I remember are *Hollow Tree Days & Nights*— about animals that lived in a hollow tree—and *Peter Rabbit*. The very best stories of all were those he made up—an ongoing saga of a community of field mice. They lived in a corn shock in the field behind his childhood home—a farm in Chittenango—and had many adventures.

The books of my childhood - I remember Nancy Drew, of course - but also *Bomba The Jungle Boy* from my brother's collection. I remember *Little Women* and *Polly-What's-Her-Name* and *The Five Little Peppers* and *Anne of Green Gables*. I even gave *Elsie Dinsmore* an earnest try but decided that the series should have been titled *Elsie Dismal*. And of course, I was devoted to the aforementioned books of Albert Payson Terhune. I was an avid reader then and remain so to this day.

The Grand & Glorious *New York World's Fair* *1939 - 40*

This event is often portrayed in historical accounts with high drama - contrasting the 'festivities' with the 'war clouds looming'. It may have

27

been *the last hurrah* - but for me, it was a wonderland full of incredible things. We went both years - using our free pass on the New York Central and staying with cousins of my mother who lived in Jamaica, Long Island. The **wonders** - Billy Rose's Aquacade starring swimmer Eleanor Holm; the magnificent *Perisphere and Trylon*; the fantastic *General Motors diorama* with a 'world of the future' laid out before us!

My brother took the 'parachute jump' ride - my mother and I were too skittish for that! I got a free pin - a tiny gherkin pickle - at the Heinz pavilion and we sampled a *'wonderful'* new spread called *oleo-margarine* (pronounced **marger-een**). My mother declared that it was 'very good'. A couple years later - when it was forced on us by butter shortages during World War II, she denied ever saying that! The World's Fair was Disney World for us. Twenty five years later, my husband and I visited the World's Fair of 1964 which was constructed in Flushing Meadows - on the site of the first - and the memories came flooding back.

Shopping

It was the era of the big department stores. All were downtown—there was no such thing as 'the suburbs' or *Malls*. We shopped at Dey Bros, Chappells, Witherills, Edwards—all big stores owned by local families whose names the stores bore. Flahs—owned by the Flah family—and The Addis Company (named after God-knows-what) were the premier specialty stores for women. Their merchandise was higher end and beautifully displayed - and the Addis silver foil boxes with red ribbons were the most prized under the tree at Christmas.

When it came to groceries—the only games in town—other than small neighborhood stores—were the huge A&P - as the Atlantic & Pacific Tea Company was known - and the somewhat smaller Mohican Market. They were the earliest version of the so-called 'super-market'. We still did most of our buying at the neighborhood meat markets, bakeries & small grocery stores but occasionally made forays to the A&P. I remember stopping there with my mother and coming out with four full bags—a week's groceries to take to the Adirondacks. It cost a lot—$5 for all four bags…..

Our meat most frequently came from small neighborhood meat markets. Usually, we shopped at Wagners, a market on the German North side..

The floors were covered with immaculate appearing sawdust and the owner, George Wagner, inevitably presented us children with a large slice of baloney - a real treat.

The War Years

Oddly, I don't have a distinct recollection of that fateful Sunday – December 7, 1941 when I was ten. I do have a vague memory of a pall descending on our home on that day – a feeling of dis-ease that enveloped the house. Of course. My brother, Jack, was twenty years old and attending Syracuse University, where he was a member of ROTC.

He and his friends made haste to enlist in what was then known as the Army Air Corps. There was no separate Air Force then—it was just a branch of the regular Army. Jack was shipped to Fort Niagara for induction, then to Miami Beach for Basic Training. No – that's not a misprint. The Air Corps had taken over all the large luxury hotels in Miami Beach and housed the trainees in them.

Jack had undergone induction at Fort Niagara and been shipped to Miami when —suddenly—there was a brief flurry of government activity. His induction x-rays had caught up to him and

they revealed scars on his lungs! As it turned out, they were scars left from his tuberculosis infection at the age of four, which was successfully treated at home. It was not a recurrence. My parents, of course, hoped that the scars would render him unfit for service and he would get a medical discharge. He – on the other hand – was hoping for the opposite. His wish was granted – he stayed in the Air Corps and our front window continued to be adorned with a small red bordered flag with a blue star on a white field – the symbol of a family member in service.

Jack - at left - in Kansas...

Later – much to his chagrin and my mother's great joy – he was disqualified both for Officers Candidate School (though his ROTC training put him on track for it) and overseas duty – because his vision without glasses was so poor, even in those days when they accepted anything that breathed and walked. The military stated that if he lost his glasses in battle he wouldn't be able to tell friend from foe! So my brother wound up as a Weather Observer – 'fighting' the entire war in Liberal, Kansas where the chief enemy was boredom. Few of the photos of that time show him - or me - wearing glasses. In those days, we all took them off for photos - even though it left us with those peculiar 'raccoon' white circles around our eyes in summer!

Wartime Travel

My father's railroad employment became a great asset during those war years because my mother and I were able to travel to see Jack without any cost. We had a pass for the New York Central and railroad employees could get a pass for out-of-state railroad lines simply by applying for it. My father had to work but my mother and I visited Jack both in Miami Beach and – later – in Grand Rapids, Michigan – where he was enrolled in the Air Corps Weather School.

Travel by car was severely restricted. First of all – all new car production was halted and the plants were completely converted to military production. No new cars were manufactured during the four years of the war. Second - gas was strictly rationed. Cards were issued which were labeled A, B & C – denoting the importance of the use of that car and how much gas was allotted. I checked the specifics online and found the following at a web site called "The Straight Dope":

30

"How was gas rationing handled during World War II? Poorly. Actually, gas wasn't what they were rationing at all. The main purpose of the restrictions on gas purchasing was to conserve tires. (And you thought those bureaucrats were stupid.) Japanese armies in the Far East, you see, had cut the U.S. off from its chief supply of rubber. There were four rationing classifications. An "A" classification, which could be had by almost anyone, entitled the holder to four gallons a week. A "B" classification was worth about eight gallons a week. "C" was reserved for important folk, like doctors, and the magic "X" went to people whose very survival required that they be able to purchase gasoline in unlimited quantities--rich people and politicians, for example. (Do I detect a wee bit of sarcasm there)? Rationing was handled through the federal Office of Price Administration. To get a classification and rationing stamps, citizens appeared at the OPA office in person and swore to the high heavens that they (1) needed gas desperately and (2) owned no more than five automobile tires (any in excess of five were confiscated by the government). Each driver was given a windshield sticker that proclaimed his classification for all the world to see. Theoretically, each gallon of gasoline sold was accounted for. The buyer surrendered his stamp at the point of purchase, and the vendor forwarded the records to the OPA. Gas rationing began on a nationwide basis on December 1, 1942. It ended on August 15, 1945. Speed limits were 35 MPH for the duration. For a short time in 1943, rations were reduced further and all pleasure driving was outlawed."

Troop trains carried soldiers en route to assignments but the civilian trains were severely taxed. I remember boarding the train for Grand Rapids when we went to visit my brother. It was evening. The train we were taking stopped in Syracuse, en-route from New York City, and it was jammed with travelers. People were standing and sitting on suitcases in the aisles. That's where my mother and I were, when a porter appeared from nowhere, touched my mother's arm, called her by name and murmured "Please follow me". It seems that my father had put the word out that we were to be 'looked after'. The porter shepherded us back to the empty dining car where he seated us at a table to spend the night. I remember putting my head down on the table on my folded arms – as we did during rest time in school – and that we were exceedingly grateful....

On the return trip from Grand Rapids, we did find seats – and as we waited in the station, a troop train pulled in on the opposite track. There was a baggage cart on the platform and a black redcap (as baggage handlers were called) leaped onto the cart and proceeded to do a fantastic tap dance routine for the cheering soldiers. It was so unreal – like a scene from a Hollywood movie! I have never forgotten it.

Prior to the Grand Rapids trip, my mother and I traveled to Miami Beach by train to visit my brother while he was in Basic Training. The trains on that trip were not as crowded but accommodations in Miami Beach were severely restricted - only small residential hotels on side streets were available. Even the - at that time - renowned Roney Plaza Hotel on the beach had been commandeered by the Air Corps to house the troops. I'm pictured here with a little boy who was also there with his family – also visiting his brother. I remember his name was 'Louie', he was from the Midwest – and

we became great pals – exploring on our own to a degree that would be unthinkable today!

We were awakened early each morning by soldiers turned out for drill. They would sing/chant in cadence as they marched. At night, we were required to draw heavy blackout curtains at the windows so that submarines lurking off coast would not have the city lights to silhouette our ships moving along the coast. By day, dirigibles prowled overhead to spot the shadows of marauding German subs in the off-shore waters. Curiously, I never wanted to return to Miami Beach. I always felt that I didn't want to see that place, filled with such vitality and such a sense of community in the war years, occupied by *tourists*....

The Mysterious Passenger

My father's work pattern as a railroad conductor in those days was to work two days and then be off duty for two days. There were no paid vacations or holidays – including Christmas Day. (After all – they only worked half the year and employees spending time with family was not a high priority). I remember many Christmases when my father was absent

– or had to go to work on Christmas Eve or Christmas Day.

One day when Dad was home, the phone rang. In very tense tones, he was told to report for work in his very best uniform with all the buttons polished – and he was not to tell anyone – under any circumstances! There would be a very special passenger aboard a special train. We were possessed with excitement. *Surely it was President Roosevelt!* My mother and I went to the movies that evening. I remember looking up at the silhouetted gargoyles that bordered the ceiling of the rococo Loews State Theater in downtown Syracuse, and wondering if it was indeed the president!

As it turned out, it was *Winston Churchill.* He had arrived in Canada and entered this country secretly to meet with President Roosevelt in Washington.

The War Effort

War Bonds were issued and sold to fund the war effort. The minimum face value of a bond was $25 – it cost $18.75 and could be redeemed for $25 in ten years! There were War Bond rallies where celebrities from the entertainment world appeared and promoted the sales. (It was while returning from such a rally that Carole Lombard, actress/comedienne and wife of Clark Gable, was killed in an airplane crash). Radio entertainers signed off their programs with the words *"Bye-bye – Buy Bonds!"*

We children bought War Bond stamps in school. We received booklets into which we pasted the them. When $18.75 in stamps accumulated, the books could be traded in for a bond. I don't recall that anyone ever reached that goal.

Not only was gas rationed – so were meat & butter. Stamps were issued by the OPA - Office for Price Administration - for such consumables. Imagine the outcry today – but no one complained. Much. We were all in the same boat – and those who cheated were looked down upon. People donated brass beds and many such metal objects to the war effort. Used 'tinfoil' was saved and donated. Conservation was a much used word.

Margarine, to which we were introduced at the World's Fair, replaced butter. It came in a solid pound block and was white, looking much like lard. The package also contained a clear bag and a bright orange capsule. We put the margarine and capsule in the bag and *kneaded* it until the margarine took on a uniform yellow hue. This tedious business was the result of lobbying by the dairy industry in order to put margarine at a disadvantage with butter.

Almost everyone had a Victory Garden – in their backyard or a nearby vacant lot. Some people even kept chickens in their back yard – though roosters were definitely frowned upon! In our case, there were extensive fields across the street from our house. There, many of the neighbors planted their gardens. My father's garden was huge. He was brought up on a farm – and how he loved that garden. He grew so much produce that we had trouble giving away the excess!

My bed was by a window and – at night – I could look up and see the sky. Often there would be the drone of a plane overhead, its lights portentous against the dark sky. It was always military, of course. Nothing else flew in those days – and there were no jets so the sound was quite different. Not a roar – but a pulsating drone – almost rhythmic as its lights moved slowly across the visible area of sky. Each time I saw one, I would say a prayer for the soldiers I knew were aboard—and I was filled with a profound sadness and loneliness.

I'd lie in bed and listen to the little plastic Motorola radio on my bedside stand. I had to be careful to turn it off if I heard steps coming up the stairs because I listened much later that I was supposed to – well past my 'lights out' time. I most particularly remember listening to Bob Hope's program and there is a distinct memory of lying there alone in the dark, in the first few months of the war – when things were going so badly – and being deathly afraid that the 'Japs' were going to invade California! It was a fearful time to be eleven years old.

There was no television to bring the war into our living rooms—but there were the newsreels at the movies— sandwiched between the 'double features', cartoons, 'short subjects' and Coming Attractions. There—in a darkened theater, we saw the endless shots of planes firing upon each other, ships being bombed. To this day, I become exceedingly nervous when I see such scenes on the History channel or in old movies.

It was toward the end of the war, that we saw the newsreel pictures of the emaciated American soldiers from Bataan who had been taken prisoner by the Japanese and so horribly mistreated—and the even more horrifying pictures - in newsreels and Life magazine - of General Eisenhower and his soldiers wending their way around huge mounds of skeletal naked bodies in the German death camps.

Jack & Sallie on Jack's winter of '43 furlough ~ Christmas Day ~

My brother's furloughs were occasions for rejoicing. For their duration, life seemed almost normal again. He had never been 'mean' to me but often ignored and bossed me about in the critical manner of an older sibling. I—on the other hand— liked to tease him in the immemorial fashion of a sister ten years younger. Now—there was a kindness and a sort of tenderness evident in our treatment of each other.

I have a photo of the two of us - taken when Jack was home on his first Christmas furlough in 1943—I was 12— he was 22. We're standing in front of our house—he in his uniform and me in my brown "Teddy Bear coat"—which was all the rage for young teens that year!

It was in 1945—when the war was drawing to a close—that President Roosevelt died. My mother and I were downtown and happened to go into a drugstore. Shocked looking people were crowded around the counter where a radio was blasting out the news that the president had died. I remember that I felt a terrible emptiness—it was as though I had received word that my father was dead. Roosevelt became president when I was one year old and was president all those years that I was 'growing up'. Everyone shared the same look of loss and confusion…

Where There's Smoke…

Sophistication was a cigarette! We viewed the great screen stars—the manly men, the svelte women—as they moved seductively through a haze of exhaled smoke. Years later, many of these luminaries died

35

prematurely of lung cancer or emphysema. Stars of the 40's such as John Wayne, Humphrey Bogart, Robert Taylor, Anne Miller—to name just a few. We saw actors in commercials and in magazines, wearing white coats and stethoscopes, telling us that 9 out of 10 doctors smoked Lucky Strike or Camels or whatever—and of course we believed. We saw the Marlboro Man astride his horse and believed. The cigarette companies did their part for the war effort by sending cases of cigarettes to "our boys in the Armed Services". Smoking was a rite of passage. Almost everyone I knew smoked to some extent. I had my first cigarette in High School. I was one of the lucky ones—I never really enjoyed it. I never got hooked. Today—very few people in our generation who *did* get hooked are still alive. Everyone I know in their 60s, 70s and 80s—and in reasonably good health—gave up smoking many years ago. Those few dedicated smokers who *are* still alive show the ravages of years of smoking—hacking coughs, hoarse voices, premature wrinkling—and are often connected to an oxygen tank by plastic umbilical cords. I know all that—and I know smoking killed many people I knew and many of that great generation of stars—but I still feel a jolt of recognition and nostalgia when viewing those old movies….

The Post-War Years - High School and College

My mother, brother & me - I was 15 or 16.

We survived those times. We were fortunate—no one close to us lost a son or a family member, when so many others did. My cousin, Harold Whitham, Jr. was a Marine who fought in the Pacific. He endured every major landing from Guadalcanal on and earned a silver star for bravery. It was amazing that he came home without even being wounded, but he did not escape unscathed. His mother would often find him in bed in the morning with his back against the headboard and his head resting on his knees, in the characteristic foxhole position. She knew that it would not be wise to wake him suddenly or with a touch....

My brother came home to a changing world. Veterans were returning in vast numbers and taking advantage of all the special programs provided them in thanks for what they had done and what they had given up. They went to college on the G.I. Bill that had such a huge impact on our generation, bought homes with low interest loans, married and had children ... and more children.... and more. It was the end of The Depression and the beginning of the Baby Boom. My brother went back to college – this time on the GI Bill – changing his Major from Liberal Arts to Business Administration... and I went on to High School.

In that era, the Syracuse schools were divided into *Elementary*—grades K thru 6, *Junior High*—grades 7 thru 9 and *Senior High*—grades 10 through 12. I attended Nottingham High School in Syracuse. It was on the opposite side of town but at that time we could attend the school of our choice. My best friend from Junior High was going to go to Nottingham – so that settled it. Of course, we darned well had to get there on our own. No school buses transported us. We boarded the city bus each morning, buying tokens - and got a 'transfer' to another bus line that serviced the area where the school was located. We rode downtown, waited on a corner – no matter what the weather – and caught another scheduled bus that took us to our destination.

We did not consider it a hardship. Indeed – it was a congenial group that met each morning and reversed the procedure each afternoon. On the

ME ON MY LUNCH HOUR –
CLINTON SQUARE - SYRACUSE

way home, I and my friends often stopped at Schrafft's Restaurant soda fountain. My treat of choice was a chocolate ice cream soda with coffee ice cream. Sometimes we went to Kirtland's, the premier stationery store in downtown Syracuse. To this day, I have carried on a love affair with such places but now they go by names such as OfficeMax and Staples....

After I turned sixteen, I had summer jobs in - variously - local stores and banks. Everyone worked summers – it was just what you did and those who didn't were rather looked down upon. The city streets were always packed with people – the city was a vibrant place – because it was the only place to shop. Shopping, however, was not such a big deal - we shopped when we needed things – school clothes, Christmas presents - whatever.

Even then, though – there were fads. When I was in High School every girl had a camel hair coat. On the bitterest, gusty winter days it was the custom to leave them unbuttoned and flying in the wind – but we always wore head scarves – folded in triangular shape and tied under the chin. (For the record, I wouldn't be caught dead wearing headgear like that today).

Shoe fads came and went. There was always the saddle shoe - (*see photo*) - of course. For a time, moccasin-type loafers were the rage. Both were worn with oversize, bulky white ankle socks that sagged around the ankle. The de rigueur school day garb was a wool cardigan style sweater worn backwards – buttoned down the back – with a

string of costume pearls and often with a white dickey. The skirts were knee length, wool and had 'box' pleats for the most part. Then, as now - blue jeans were popular—but with the legs rolled up. One leg was rolled just below the knee and the other just below that. (Never the same length). These 'couture' items were worn with a man's shirt – looted from our brothers' and fathers' closets and worn un-tucked! However, we were not allowed to wear jeans in school.

Photos: *Above: High School sorority dance*
Right: *Me in the dress I wore for graduation - (caps & gowns were not worn then - at least in our school)*

Hair styles were a bit better than during the war and the pre-war years. Gone were the pompadours and snoods worn by the slightly older girls at that time. Our age group wore hair long and – most often – in a pageboy. We rolled our hair under at night using old socks, rags or fat metal curlers.

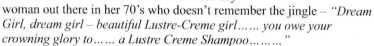

Most girls washed their hair on Thursday night. That was to give the impression that we had a big date on Friday – which usually wasn't true at all - at least for me. Is there any woman out there in her 70's who doesn't remember the jingle – *"Dream Girl, dream girl – beautiful Lustre-Creme girl…… you owe your crowning glory to…… a Lustre Creme Shampoo………"*

Dating— it was the best of times and the worst of times. There were virtually no 'free agents'. You either went steady—or you didn't go out—except on blind dates. Occasionally, a 'couple' would break up and the male half would start scouting for new talent but it was unheard of for girls to ask boys out—except to sorority dances. Then, it was permitted. In fact – it was *required,* a fact that made 'going steady' a sort of 'social security', i.e. no frantic efforts to garner a date!

Going steady did not necessarily mean sex—though unquestionably a lot of 'heavy breathing' took place in parked cars. It was not a subject that was discussed—at least among us girls. The female world was divided into 'good girls' and those who 'did it' - and there apparently weren't a lot of the latter. God knows—people wouldn't brag about it. Girl-type people anyway. After all - one had one's *reputation* to consider. I was one of those who never had what I considered a 'real date' until college. Being 'fixed up' with a date didn't count. It was a relatively innocent and undemanding era. By the time we embarked on 'serious' dating, we were old enough to have at least *some* idea who we were.

The College Years

I graduated from Nottingham in 1949 – the same year my brother, whose college was delayed by his war service, graduated from Syracuse. We didn't have to make a commitment to college early and college was easy to get into if you could afford the tuition. SATs were called *College Entrance Examinations.* New York State had—and has—what are called Regents Exams. Graduation depended on getting a minimum grade of 65. In order to get into college, a minimum grade of 75 was required. Most girls of that era, pushed by parents and counselors, drifted into Liberal Arts, Education or Home Economics. I headed to Syracuse University's College of Fine Arts, (now the College of Visual & Performing Arts - or VPA).

In those days, all you really needed for college acceptance - almost anywhere – were passing grades and a tuition check in your hand. I had both – plus an acceptable portfolio of art work, assembled in High School. I was accepted and started college in the fall of 1949. The tuition – not including room and board – was the staggering sum of $250 per semester. The following (spring) semester, it was raised to $275 because of increasing costs…

Crouse - the great stone gothic 'castle' that housed the College of Fine Arts – as it was then called, (later the College of Visual & Performing Arts) – was a wonderful place.

(I took this photo of the parapets of Crouse College in 1950 with my Kodak 'Brownie' camera). Its interior was all wood—the walls, floors and ornate carved staircases. The place was permeated with the smell of turpentine. It was a wonder it didn't go up in flames, considering that most students – and faculty – smoked in those days. We would gather in the hallways before class and during breaks, turning the air blue with smoke.

The campus in general, though, was a bit of a mess – with Quonset huts and Army 'pre-fabs' housing many of the classes and administrative offices. This was due to the unprecedented influx of veterans attending colleges under the GI Bill, following the war. Most of my classes were in these temporary quarters the first year. (Freshmen were pretty low in the pecking order).

I'm at the left in this group shot of my classmates taking a break during our General Drawing class. We're outside one of those pre-fabs that housed classes for a few years after the war. The buildings remained in use for several years

The art students were the only people who were allowed to wear jeans to class – because of the various messy media used. (Acrylic paint had not yet come into use – oil paint prevailed). Fine Artists could always be

identified on campus because they were the only students wearing jeans. There were times when we girls wore skirts simply because we got tired of the same old thing. I pretty much stopped that after sitting on a palette of wet oil paint one day, while wearing a favorite tweed skirt..

I went through 'rushing' and joined a sorority, but never lived on campus. *(At left- wearing my 'pledge pin').* We

41

lived about two miles from campus and I walked almost every day, preferring that to taking the bus with the need to 'transfer'. Our art classes were 'labs' that lasted three hours, so - many times in winter - I walked home in the snowy darkness after a two PM to five PM class, often carrying a large portfolio of work.

During the second year of Art School, we were finally 'allowed' to take 'real' painting classes. (The assumption was that we learned the basics during the first year). I developed an immediate affinity for the watercolor medium - its freshness and spontaneity.

This still life - was the first watercolor painting I did in class. My instructor, Margaret Boehner — who was nearing retirement and was very 'old school' - looked at it after I had done *the initial drawing* and had laid in some rather pallid and timid washes. She took my brush and proceeded to paint in the strong bold contrasts. Painting into a student's painting is a teaching 'no-no' today—and was even then—but she made a point I've never forgotten. I still have the painting (at left). I love it but I never signed it, since I considered it more her work than mine.

In the spring, we art students would fan out into the neighborhood carrying our paraphernalia and stopping to paint whatever interested us. Ever since then, I think of spring as *"the watercolor season"* - with 'washes' of pale green splashed on the tree branches. The two landscape paintings pictured here are from (rather inadequate) old Kodacolor pictures taken of some of my first paintings, done in spring of 1951. The trio of Victorian houses was on the northwest corner of Irving and Adams Streets in Syracuse and they are long gone now, as is the other house—which was on Comstock Avenue. These paintings were truly 'mine'. I sold one and gave the other to a friend many years ago.

I completed two years of college and became engaged in 1951 to my future husband, Dwight Bailey. He had joined the Air Force during the Korean War (just prior to being drafted). I decided to work full time and save for our future while he did the same during his two years of overseas duty in Libya. Much later, after the birth of our children, I took additional college art courses at Syracuse University College, joined an art guild and thus began a long career as a professional artist.

A Montage of Family Photos from the 30's & 40's

Clockwise from top: me in my English pram; on the beach at Green Lakes State Park with my mother (note her beach garb – including *stockings*); natty in navy blue; Aunt Ethel with me & little friend; riding a pony at a friend's house.

Upper left – I'm wearing a locket given to me when I was seven – I gave it to our granddaughter when she turned seven; Dad working on our '39 Buick; motel/cabin accommodations in the '30s; the house where we were living when war broke out – probably taken summer of '42…

At age 11(called the awkward age) -with my grandmother - and age 12 & age 13 (with my beloved pets, our cat Butch and collie pup, Lad).

16 years

14 years

46

Forestview Camp – me, Mom, Aunt Lena, Dad, Uncle Hugh

Jack & me – Bald Mt - summer of '47

Mom & I & 49 (?) Chrysler

Jack, Aunt Ethel, Uncle Clinton,
me and Momma – Family Picnic
at Aunt Ethel's home

My engagement announced...

Fashions of the 40's & Early 50's

My brother's shirt – with jeans; Saddle shoes or loafers & the new longer skirt

LEFT: Easter Sunday - me with friend Carol & Right: With friend Barbara, wearing my favorite Jonathan Logan dress – forest green with white piping. It was expensive, too - about fifteen dollars.

*I met my future husband, Dwight, in 1950 - we were married July 10, 1954. I have no records of the cost of our 1954 wedding - but when you consider that a 1954 Plymouth cost about $1,600 (gas by the way was 22 cents a gallon) and the average cost for a house was $10,250, you can probably estimate the amount. My wedding gown had been worn previously by my brother's wife **and** her sister. Wedding garb is perhaps the only thing that hasn't changed too much over the years. While modern gowns may be more sophisticated, they co-exist with 'frou-frou' gowns adorned with lace and ruffles.*

1954

1954

2004

This brings me to the end of this portion of my story. Still to come were children and grandchildren - and that's 'a whole other story'.

Addendum: Additional Photos
from the '30s, '40's and '50's

Saltie & Eugene

Salem Hyde School - left

My brother and I - above - the hat he wears was called a 'Skippy' hat - after the comic strip character who wore one. As I recall, it was made of felt. You'll also note his knickers and argyle type knee socks that were worn with knickers.

Eugene and me - I was eight years old when we lived briefly on Westmoreland Avenue in the university section of Syracuse

West Moreland St. House Note Snow drifts

51

I remember when the picture at left was taken. It was the summer between high school and college - summer of 1949 - and I was wondering what lay ahead. I remember feeling very lonely and adrift that day and I think you can see it in the photo...

At top right: my mother and I sitting on the bumper of our 1951(?) Chrysler.

Bottom right: I and three friends at Methodist Camp/ Conference Center, Casowasco - 1952 or 1953. The camp was, and still is, on Owasco Lake.

Top Left: Dwight - stationed in Libya during the Korean War.

Top Right: I was perched on the hood of a 'civilian' Jeep at Casowasco

Bottom Right: In summer of 1953, the year before my marriage, my parents took me and a friend on a trip through New England. This photo was taken by Plymouth Rock and is an accurate picture of what we wore to travel then: *a dress, stockings & heels!* We were traveling by car but didn't wear shorts or slacks except when we spent a night in the White Mountains and Adirondacks on our way home! Then they were acceptable.

Afterword

The following is a case in point about why it is important for you to ask questions while those whom you can ask are still alive. I was told that my great-grandmother was French Canadian; that when she and her husband first came to this country they lived in a dirt floored cabin near Oswego, New York.

I never saw a photograph of her - or even knew one existed - until a cousin showed me a picture from one of her own family albums. There is no mistaking the ethnic background of the woman with the intricately beaded collar and sober mien; no doubt about that of the unknown child at her side. This discovery came long after my mother's death. There was no one left to whom I could address my many questions - no answers to be had.

At left: My Great-Grandmother, Kate LaClair Loungley (Longley/ Loungliere) & Unknown Child

The silence seems impenetrable. What were my great-grandmother's origins - and by extension - mine? I can't reach her. She's carefully hidden from view by the traditions of shame that were felt by later generations. I look in the mirror and the face that looks back at me holds no clue.

History notes that most of the very early settlers of Canada were French *men* - immigrants who became traders and trappers. There was seldom friction between the native Indians and the trappers, since the latter had little interest in taking the land for homesteading and farming, as was the purpose of the English colonists to the south. Few of the trappers, if any, brought wives or daughters with them and many of them entered into marriages, or quasi-marriages, with Indian women. The trappers were called *coureurs du bois* - literally - 'runners of the woods'.

About the author: Sallie Naatz Bailey is a free lance artist and writer who was born in Syracuse, NY in 1931. She graduated from Nottingham High School and studied art at Syracuse University. Bailey has worked in many media including serigraphs, watercolor & original computer prints. In addition to the places listed in the resume, her work has been shown at the Roberson Arts Center, Binghamton, NY; the Legislative Office Building, Albany, NY; Selected Artists Gallery, Utica, NY; Limestone Gallery of Fayetteville; the Manlius Library Art Gallery, East Village Arts Gallery in E. Syracuse, NY and the Everson Museum Sales Gallery, Syracuse, NY. She is a past president and board member of both the Associated Artists of Syracuse and the Central New York Branch of the National League of American Pen Women.

Her work has received many awards, including the Associated Artists' Gordon Steele Best in Show medal twice. It is in the permanent collections - via purchase prizes - of the Community Arts Center of Old Forge, NY, plus those of 'the banks formerly known as' KeyBank, Chase, Lincoln First, Fleet and Marine Midland. She is also represented in many corporate and private collections, has done illustrations for *Blueline,* a literary magazine, and has designed stencil patterns for Saltbox Studios of Massachusetts and The Shade Tree of Manlius, NY.

Bailey authored numerous guest columns on the Art Page of the *Syracuse Newspapers Sunday Stars* section during the 70's, was art reviewer for several years for the *Eagle Bulletin,* a prize winning weekly newspaper serving the eastern suburbs of Syracuse and has had articles in the *Adirondack Echo,* the magazine *New York Alive, The Healing Muse* and *Lake Effect,* a literary journal published in Oswego, NY. Her poems have been published in several small magazines, including the *Comstock Review* and *Alura.* She also authored the segment on the art history of the Central New York region in the *Encyclopedia of New York State* and did the jacket design for the novel, *Swimming Toward The Light,* published in 2007 by Syracuse University Press. Her essay, *The Accidental Therapists* will appear in the 2009 edition of *The Healing Muse,* published by Upstate Medical University.

Made in the USA